DROP SHIPPING

Blueprint to $10k a Month! – Comprehensive Guide to Private Label, Retail Arbitrage, and Finding Profitable Products

By: Greg Addison

Free Bonus: Join Our Book Club and Receive Free Gifts Instantly

Click Below For Your Bonus:

https://success321.leadpages.co/freebodymindsoul/

TABLE OF CONTENTS

INTRODUCTION

Anyone who wants to start his or her own retail business faces quite a few challenges. Sufficient capital, the complexities of starting out, and high overhead expenses are just a few of the challenges that can turn into major stumbling blocks if you try to venture into retail. The question arises – is there any way that you can somehow reduce the scope of these factors and still be able to break through into retail?

The answer is yes! Of course, you can. What the means to this end is drop shipping. A retail method that doesn't require a huge amount of capital investment is easy to start and cuts down on overhead expenses; drop shipping is not a recent phenomenon. The fact is that it has been around for some time now and it is your turn to take advantage of what it offers to the retailer just starting out.

Read on to find out exactly what drop shipping is. In this book, I will discuss the players involved in this arena, what the process is, and how you can start your own drop shipping enterprise. I will also tell you how to identify the most reliable suppliers and how to pick the best products for you to drop ship. Additionally, I will cover how you can determine which sales channel is best for you and how you can best run your drop shipping business.

So what are you waiting for? Go ahead, get started and I wish you all the best!

CHAPTER ONE

UNDERSTANDING DROP SHIPPING

Before you start a drop shipping business, the most basic thing you'll need to know is what the business is all about and who the major players involved are. So, without further ado, let's begin.

What is Drop Shipping?

Well, the first thing to note here is that it is not dropping off supplies and/or cargo on a ship somewhere in the middle of the ocean. Now that we've got that straight let's get some basic terminology right too. You may have heard people saying that they want to do drop shipping or start a drop shipping business. While, in common parlance, we may understand what they mean, you need to be very clear that if you venture into this field, you are **not** the drop shipper. When someone says that they want to start drop shipping, what they're really saying is that they want to become retailers who use drop shipping suppliers.

Drop shipping is a way of retail fulfillment in which the store involved doesn't stock products that it sells. Wholesalers (well, some of them) offer a drop shipping service. When you, as a retailer, have an agreement with a wholesaler who offers such a service, you don't have to take on the shipping or stocking the inventory. When you sell the product to the customer, you buy the product from the wholesaler who ships the product to the customer directly. You never see or stock the product. This means that you don't have to worry about storage, shipping costs or any of the overheads that come with a regular retail business.

Drop Shipping: Role or Service?

Although you may have heard the term 'drop shipper' bandied about quite freely, the truth is that no such term actually exists in this field. There is no one person or entity who can be a drop shipper. Anyone in the supply chain – the wholesaler, the retailer or even the manufacturer – can be the drop shipper.

If the manufacturer you are working with ships the goods directly to the customer, once you've placed an order with them, the manufacturer 'drop ships' on your behalf. In the same way, another retailer also has the capability to drop ship for you: although, in this case, your profit margin may not be as high. A retailer's pricing is going to be higher than a wholesaler's or a manufacturer's.

This brings us to the fact that merely because an entity says that it is a 'drop shipper' doesn't mean that they will offer you wholesale pricing. All it means is that the business is willing to ship the products to you. Therefore, if you want to get the best possible pricing, you need to ensure that you work directly with a manufacturer or wholesaler. I will discuss this in more detail in a later chapter.

The Players

To understand the major players involved in drop shipping, you need first to understand what is meant by the term 'supply chain'. The term basically means the course followed by a product from inception to manufacturing to the customer. Those who look at the supply chain in detail state that the supply chain of a product actually begins from the basic materials such as rubber and oil that are mined to create it. For the purposes of this book, we need only look at the players involved in the drop shipping supply chain.

Manufacturers – The ones who create the product are the manufacturers. They don't generally sell to the public directly but do sell their product to retailers and wholesalers in bulk quantities.

The most inexpensive way to buy products to sell them to the public is to go to the manufacturers. However, many of them have minimum requirements for purchase that you'll need to satisfy. Also, you will need to do the stocking and shipping when you sell the products to your customers. That is why it is generally easier and more cost-effective to buy the products from wholesalers.

Wholesalers – The ones who buy the products from the manufacturers, increase the price by a small margin and then sell the products to the retailers are known as wholesalers. Not all of them have minimum requirements when it comes to purchases, and even if they do, those requirements are fairly easy for you to meet.

A wholesaler will not generally limit itself to one manufacturer, but instead, they buy and stock products from many different manufacturers. However, it does limit itself to a specific niche. For example, a clothing wholesaler will not purchase and sell cellular phones. Most of these companies only deal in wholesale and don't sell to the public.

Retailers – One who sells the products to the public after marking up the price is known as a retailer. Therefore, if you have a drop shipping agreement with a wholesaler or manufacturer and you sell the products to the customers, you are a retailer.

How Drop Shipping Works

Now that we've taken a look at the players in this chain let's see how the whole process works. To make this easy for you to understand, I'll create an example using a hypothetical store called Electronics Showroom which is an online entity that sells electronics such as laptops and cell phones to the public. Electronics Showroom has a drop shipping agreement for its products with a wholesaler that I'll call Wholesale Electronics.

Below is an example of how the process will work.

1. Electronics Showroom receives an order from the customer.

Mr. Smith places an online order for a laptop via Electronics Showroom's online store. The order is approved. This is what happens next.

Both Mr. Smith and Electronics Showroom receive emails confirming the order. The store's software usually generates the email confirmation automatically.

When Mr. Smith checks out, his payment is captured by the store's payment software, which then deposits the payment into Electronics Showroom's bank account.

2. Electronics Showroom places the order with Wholesale Electronics

Generally, this is done by Electronics Showroom forwarding the email confirmation to Wholesale Electronics. Since Wholesale Electronics will have Electronics Showroom's credit card information, it will bill the card for the wholesale price of the laptop and include any other fees such as the shipping fee.

While email is the usual way of placing an order, there are wholesalers who allow for the order to be placed online manually or use XML order uploading.

3. The order is shipped out by Wholesale Electronics

If the laptop is in stock and the credit card belonging to Electronics Showroom is successfully billed, the order is packed up and shipped directly to the customer by Wholesale Electronics. Now, the important thing to note here is that, although it is Wholesale Electronics doing the shipping, the name and address on the return address label will be that of Electronics Showroom. The same will also be seen on the packing slip and invoice. When the shipment has been sent out, an invoice and tracking number is sent to Electronics Showroom by Wholesale Electronics.

While, in the past, there have been some concerns about the turnaround time for the shipping when it comes to dropping shipped orders, in actuality, this is much faster than you may believe. Suppliers who have a good reputation normally ship out the product within a few hours of receiving the order. This means that even if you use a drop ship supplier, you can still promise next day delivery.

4. The customer is notified of the shipment by Electronics Showroom

Once it receives the tracking number, Electronics Showroom sends that information to Mr. Smith. Mostly this is done through an email interface which is built into the interface of the online store. Now that the payment has been collected, the order shipped and the customer is informed thus the process is now complete. The difference between the price that Electronics Showroom paid to Wholesale Electronics and charged Mr. Smith would be its profit or loss.

Customers Don't See Drop Shippers

In effect, drop shippers don't exist for the customer. Although the role that the drop shipper plays is crucial in the entire process, it is Electronics Showroom's logo, name, and address that the customer sees on the label of the shipment. If Mr. Smith gets a faulty laptop, he will get in touch with Electronics Showroom. It would then get in touch with Wholesale Electronics to get a different laptop shipped out.

The only responsibility that the drop shipping wholesaler has is to ship and stock products. The customer has no awareness of the wholesaler. The retailer has to take responsibility for the rest of it – from marketing to website development to customer service.

Reasons Why People Consider Drop Shipping

Drop Shipping is considered to be one of the businesses that people choose because of some of the advantages which include the following:

1. Wider Array of Products Ready to be sold - A drop

Since the drop shipping company does not have to purchase all of the items before the items are going to get shipped, it does not have to search for a place where the different items are going to be placed. This will help offer a lot of different products to customers.

2.   Reduction of Risk

No matter what type of business is going to be opened, it always comes with a certain risk, but when it comes to drop shipping, all of the risks that may come hand in hand with starting an online company becomes reduced significantly. For example, a drop shipping business owner does not have to worry about the items that are left unsold somewhere. There would not be any problem with storing unsold items as well.

3.   No Large Capital Needed

One of the reasons why people decide not to push through with any business is because of the large capital that they have to release. Some people do not have it while others do not want to take any risk. When it comes to dropping shipping, a large capital is not needed in order to start the business. The "drop shipper" only has to purchase an item when an order has been sent by a customer.

4.   Ability to Run the Business Anywhere

One of the problems with having any business is that the business owner may have to rent office space and spend a lot of money on renting the different items. Through a drop shipping business, the business owner may start and operate a business from anywhere as long as the person has a PC/laptop and fast internet connection.

5.   No Need to Manually Do Each Order

All of the orders that will be done through the drop shipping company's website will be easy to fulfil because the orders do not have to be written manually.

Of course, if all of the things that are mentioned above will be considered by people, then everyone may want to start a drop shipping business, but there are some disadvantages too that makes people stop for a while and rethink if they would like to start a drop shipping business or not.

1.   Low Margins - One of the biggest problems that may be experienced by anyone who would like to start a drop shipping

business is that there are a lot of people who may do this as well. For example, if you would start your own company, people may check out your website, but they will always compare it with another drop shipping company. If you would not have low prices, you will not be noticed. At the same time, if you would lower your prices too much, you will not make any profit.

2.   Some Issues with Shipping - Since drop shipping companies usually get their items from different suppliers, the price of shipping tend to be different depending on the supplier where the item will come from. This can be complicated at times because there is a need to create a uniform shipping fee for all of the items. Of course, you may have the option not to have a uniform shipping fee if you would please. It will be discussed further later on.

3.   Errors - Whenever the supplier sends a wrong item, it will be the drop shipping company's fault. Even if it is not the drop shipping company that fulfilled the order, they have to take responsibility for the error. Of course, it can be even harder if the suppliers are not good in fulfilling orders at all. A drop shipping company may fail if the owner does not know how to handle everything.

CHAPTER TWO

HOW TO FIND AND DEAL WITH SUPPLIERS

Now that you have a fair idea of what drop shipping is, who is involved in it and how it works, you need to know how you can find the supplier best suited for you and to work with it. Equally important, you need to know how to spot the fakes or the retail stores that pretend to be drop shippers – and there are plenty of those. In fact, knowing the difference between fake drop shippers and the real deal is absolutely crucial in your quest to make your retail business success. Remember that a wholesaler buys the product straight from the manufacturer and the pricing that it offers you is going to be much better than that offered by a retail store.

How You Can Identify the Fakes

The odds are that you will encounter a significant number of 'fake' wholesalers in your search for a legitimate drop shipper. The problem lies in the fact that the 'real' wholesalers aren't that great at marketing themselves and so it is much more difficult for you to find them. 'Fake' wholesalers take advantage of this fact and are more easily found when you search for drop shippers. You need to be very careful here.

Here are a few ways in which you can spot the fakes.

Ongoing Fee Demands – If a supplier wants to charge you an ongoing fee for ordering from them and doing business with them, the chances are that you're dealing with a fake. Real wholesalers don't ask for any type of monthly fee or membership fee or even service fee.

However, it becomes crucial here for you to know the difference between a supplier and a supplier directory. A supplier directory is a sort of an index that lists wholesale suppliers, organizes them by the products they sell and screens them to ensure that they are legitimate. Such directories do charge a fee, either ongoing or a one-time fee. Don't take this as a sign that the directory is a fake.

Selling to the Public – If a wholesale supplier is selling products to the public at what it claims are 'wholesale' prices, it is a retailer selling goods at inflated prices. If you want real wholesale pricing, you need to send in an application for a wholesale account, establish that your business is legitimate and get approval before you can place the first order.

There are, however, certain genuine fees for drop shipping that you will need to pay.

Per-Order Fees – A fee of around $2 to $5 is often charged by drop shippers. This is done on a per-order basis. Sometimes the fee can be more than the amount mentioned here. The fee generally depends on the size of the product being shipped and maybe its complexity as well. Generally, this is done because shipping a single order involves higher packing and shipping costs than shipping bulk orders.

Minimum Order Sizes – Sometimes you have to purchase a certain amount for your first order from a wholesaler. A wholesaler does this to discourage retailers who are merely 'window-shopping,' will ask them questions and place small orders thereby wasting their time but won't send any kind of significant business their way.

Obviously, this can be a problem if you're drop shipping. Say your average order size is around $200, but the wholesaler has a minimum initial order size of $1000. Naturally, you won't want to pre-order $1000 worth of products just to be able to open a drop shipping account. Therefore, what you can do in such a case is to offer the wholesaler the $1000 as a credit that they will charge against for any drop shipping orders you place. This means that you can meet the wholesaler's minimum requirement by committing to buy at least $1000 worth of products without being forced to place a single large order when you don't have the customers for it.

How to Find Wholesale Suppliers

Now that you understand how to spot the fakes let's take a look at how you search for the real thing. There are different strategies that you can use, but some are more effective than others. I have listed the strategies in decreasing order of efficacy here.

Get in Touch with the Manufacturer

This is, by far, the best way to find legitimate wholesale suppliers quickly and easily. Once you have decided what product or products you are going to sell retail, contact the manufacturer and find out from them what wholesalers they sell to. Once you have the list, you can get in touch with the wholesalers to know if they offer drop shipping and how you can set up an account with them if they do.

Remember that most wholesalers carry products from a whole range of manufacturers, not just the one you got in touch with. That means that you can source a range of products in whatever niche you have decided upon. Once you've contacted two or three top manufacturers in your niche, you won't have any trouble figuring out who the genuine wholesalers are in that niche.

Use Google

While this might seem like the most obvious and easiest thing to do, you do need to keep a few things in mind.

- **Search Exhaustively** – Remember what I said earlier about wholesalers not being great at marketing? Well, this obviously means that the top results you get aren't necessarily going to be those of the legitimate wholesalers. You may have to wade through a lot of search results before finding out that the wholesaler you're looking for is result number 76.

- **Don't Judge by the Website** – Unfortunately, the websites of genuine wholesalers aren't very well-designed either. In many cases, you might find the websites harking back to the designs of the 90's. While some wholesalers do have good websites, most of them will have homepages that are, quite frankly, cringe-worthy. That doesn't mean, though, that the wholesaler isn't reliable or reputable so don't be put off.

- **Use Different Modifiers and Lots of Them** – Most wholesalers' websites aren't SEO optimized so a simple search query may not do the trick. Instead of using something like 'laptop wholesalers' alone, try using different combinations such as laptop reseller or laptop distributor or warehouse or supplier.

Place an Order with the Competition

If, despite all of this, you have trouble finding a wholesaler, here's a time-honored trick that you can use the order from your competition. Identify a competitor who you believe might be using a drop shipper and place a small order with it. Upon getting the shipment, enter the return address into Google and see if you can find out the original shipper. You may be able to find the supplier who you can then contact.

Keep in mind that the reasons the other methods given above may not have worked are insufficient demand for the product or niche or too small a market. Try this technique out only if the others haven't worked. Don't depend on it too much.

Go to a Trade Show

This is a great way of connecting with both manufacturers and suppliers in a particular niche. You can do all the research you need to and make contacts all in one place. However, to do this, you need to have determined your niche beforehand. Also, going to a trade fair may not be possible for you for many reasons. If you do have the resources to attend, however, do so. You can make good contacts among the manufacturers and suppliers here.

Consult Directories

As mentioned earlier, directories are indexes of wholesalers arranged by niche and product. These wholesalers are screened by the directory to ensure that they are legitimate. You also need to pay fees that may be ongoing or a one-time fee. Therefore, the question arises – Should you pay for a wholesaler directory?

Well, you don't really need to, but the directories are a great way to brainstorm ideas. If you have already decided which product or niche you are going with, then member directories may not be of much help, since you'll already have used the previous methods to identify reliable suppliers. In addition, once your business is underway, you won't have much occasion to come back to the directory unless you want to find wholesalers for a different product or niche.

However, if you are still wondering which niche or product would be a good idea, these directories can be great for brainstorming. In addition, you will find a whole list of suppliers, all in one place. If you don't have much time and you don't mind paying the fee, you can definitely use the directories.

There are plenty of supplier directories out there. A few you can look at our Worldwide Brands, SaleHoo, Doba and Wholesale Central. I'm not endorsing any of them, merely giving you a few options to consider and look at.

How to Get Ready for the Suppliers

Now that you have a good list of wholesalers and want to move to the next step, you need to ensure that everything on your end is organized properly.

Become Legal – As I've said earlier, wholesalers will have minimum requirements, one of which is that your company needs to be legal before you can apply for an account. Many wholesalers wait for the customer to be approved before revealing their pricing. As such, you need to ensure that you are legally incorporated so you can see what pricing to expect.

If you only want to ask basic questions such as whether they drop ship or carry a particular brand, they won't need you to be legal. However, for anything more, your business needs to be set up and ready to go.

See How You Look to Them – Wholesalers have to deal with a lot of people who claim to have 'good business plans,' ask plenty of questions, waste a lot of the wholesalers' time but never place any orders. Therefore, don't look to them to go above and beyond to help you set up your business.

While most of them will set up a drop shipping account for you with no worries, they won't give you discount pricing or be happy if you spend a lot of time on the phone with their sales people without you having sold a thing. Your reputation will go down, and your relationship with the wholesaler will become strained.

Avoid special requests as much as possible, but if you must make one, you need to be credible. Your business plan should be definite, e.g. state similar to when you're launching your website instead of giving them vague statements about maybe starting a business in the near future. If you've had professional successes before, you need to mention them, especially if they belong to the marketing and sales realm.

The whole point here is that you need to convince the supplier that allowing your special request (which is inconvenient for them) is going to yield good results in the future with the business you bring in.

Use the Phone – Many people are afraid of picking up the phone and calling the supplier for any questions they might have. They find it a lot easier to email simply. However, the truth is that a phone call is far more likely to yield the information you require then an email is.

Remember that suppliers get a lot of calls for information, including calls from entrepreneurs just setting out. You will probably get a friendly voice on the phone that is quite willing to answer any questions you might have. A great way to eliminate any stress you might be feeling is to write down whatever questions you have before the call. This ensures that you don't forget anything vital and makes the whole call go a lot easier.

How to Find Good Suppliers

Now that you know how to search for wholesalers and what you need to do in order to be ready for them, let's look at how you can identify the good ones. Obviously, the success of your business will depend on you working with the best suppliers in the field.

Look for the following qualities when deciding which suppliers to go with.

Industry Focus and Expert Staff

The best wholesalers will have well-informed sales representatives who really know their stuff – both about the industry and about the products. Remember that it is the sales representatives who'll answer your questions. This becomes even more important if you're venturing into a niche or selling a product line that you haven't worked with before.

Dedicated Support Representatives

The good drop shippers will assign one particular representative to you, who will be responsible for taking care of your account and answering any questions or fixing any problems that you might have. There are wholesalers who don't do this, and it results in problems taking a lot longer to fix and a lot of nagging to take care of one problem. It's really vital for you to have a dedicated representative who is responsible for your account.

Expert Knowledge in the Industry

It will help if you pick out a supplier who has a lot of details about the industry from which you are going to both thrive. The supplier that you are going to pick should have extensive knowledge about the different items that they are selling. You should realize that you are going to ask them for details whenever your customer asks regarding an item or before you actually promote the item to any customer, you should have all the details ready.

Technology Investment

As I mentioned earlier, most of the wholesalers don't have great websites. However, a wholesaler who does understand the value of technology and invests well in it is a lot easier to work with. If a wholesaler has features such as a wide-ranging online catalog, real-time inventory, an order history that is searchable online and data feeds that can be customized, it helps you tremendously in organizing your business and making it more efficient.

Orders via Email

At first, this might not sound like that important a feature. However, having to place every order online manually, or worse yet, having to call every order in can get quite old, quite fast – not to mention the time was taken to process the order. Ordering via email speeds up the process quite a bit and isn't nearly as time-consuming or tedious.

Central Location

If you're operating in a large country such as the United States, you will want to use a drop shipper that is at a central location so that shipments reach customers within two to three business days. A supplier located on one of the coasts will take significantly longer to ship products to customers. If your supplier is centrally located, you can promise your customers faster delivery and potentially save some costs when it comes to shipping fees.

Efficient and Organized

There are wholesalers who maintain a competent staff and have good systems. This means that your orders are generally fulfilled without any problems. Then there are the suppliers who mess up every fifth or sixth order and cause you immense amounts of frustration. The problem here lies in the fact that you can't really judge the efficiency of a wholesaler without trying it out first. As such, it is a good idea to place few test orders to find out how the wholesaler works. It won't be comprehensive by any means, but you can get some idea. Look for:

- How the order process is handled

- How fast the products are shipped out

- How fast a follow-up with invoice and tracking information is done

- What the quality of the packing is when the product arrives

Provides a Data Feed

Are you familiar with what a data feed is? Basically, this is an update to your current inventory so that you will be familiar with all of the products and even product variants that you are trying to sell to your customers. If you are still trying to understand how it can be helpful for you, think about this example.

For instance, you have 4 products which come in 5 colors. That means that you will already have 20 product listings for those products alone. You would need to update those 20 items whenever your supplier makes changes. Changes can occur once every hour or it may only change once a day depending on the supply and demand. It will be easy if you only have four products but what if you have a thousand products? You can just imagine how time consuming this would be for you.

If you have a product data feed, you can be sure that that your data will already be changed automatically depending on your supplier. This means that you do not need to worry about the changes every hour of the day while you are operating your business. This will allow you to spend more time to explore your business and to know the different things that you can do to make your business successful.

Remember that data files usually appear in different files. You may have to be familiar with the different file types especially if you have different suppliers that will send you different ones.

How to Pay Wholesalers

You have one of two options when it comes to payment that most wholesalers will accept.

Credit Card

In the beginning, most wholesalers will ask that you pay by credit card. Even once your business begins to thrive, this is still a good option. Not only is paying by credit card convenient, since you don't have to write checks, but you also earn a lot of frequent flyer miles or reward points. Since your customer will already have paid on your website, you can purchase in large volumes using your credit card without actually being out-of-pocket.

Net Terms

Another way you can pay wholesalers is 'net terms' on the invoice. This means that you have a specific number of days to pay for the products you bought. For example, if you're on 'net 45' terms, it means that you need to pay the wholesaler within 45 days of the date of purchase. Such payments are usually made by bank draw or check.

In most cases, you will need to provide the wholesaler with credit references before it offers you net payment terms. This is only to be expected considering the wholesaler is effectively giving you credit. Be ready to be asked for credit references should you choose this method of payment.

Before You Contact Various Suppliers

Now that you have already made a choice regarding the different suppliers that you would like to check out, you have to remember that dealing with possible suppliers through the phone is always better than contacting a supplier by e-mail.

You might say that talking with a supplier over the phone can be a hard task to do especially if you find it awkward. Sending an e-mail can be easier, but your communication will be longer. There is also a bigger chance that you will misunderstand each other.

You may be tempted just to call the supplier but here are some things that you should set up first:

Make Sure That Your Business is Ready

Do you want the supplier that you are going to contact to take you seriously? This will only be done by the supplier if your business is already set up. This means that you need to already have your very own business name, your logo and even your own website. It is also best if you have also registered your business legally already so that the supplier will know that you mean business. It will also help if you have been endorsed by another person who has close ties with the supplier.

Suppliers would need to be careful too because they cannot just supply any person who would suddenly decide to start his own drop shipping company out of the blue.

Remember that You are One of Many

You are not the first business owner who has contacted the supplier for their products. If the supplier that you are trying to get is popular, you can expect that you have a lot of competition. They do not just supply everyone. They choose to depend on who they think they can create a profitable business with. You need to make sure that you will stand out from all the others. In order to stand out, you have to be definite about your plans. For example, if the supplier asks you to describe your business, say that you ARE going to open your business at a specific date instead of you MIGHT. Your choice of words will make or break a possible supplier deal.

Do not be afraid to let suppliers know if you have been successful with your past dealings because this will help them feel more at ease. Of course, if you have had failures in the past, they may check this, and it will be harder for you to find the right supplier that can fulfil your customers' order needs.

Have a List of Questions Ready

If you are phone conscious, you might end up stuttering on the phone even if this is not your intention. What you can do is you can write down a list of questions that you truly want to ask the supplier. You may even practice saying those questions so that it will not be too awkward and it will not be too obvious that you are referring to a piece of paper or a note regarding the things you are going to ask.

When you have a list of questions ready, you will have the tendency to become more formal and business like so that suppliers will know that you are seriously considering doing business with them. At the same time, you will have a lesser chance of forgetting important details that you want to ask. You do not want to sound awkward and inexperienced on the phone, right?

A Shortcut to Finding the Right Supplier

Of course, even business owners would like to take the easy way from time to time because who actually want to go through a long and lengthy process of finding a supplier when it can be done easily?

You can partner with a channel that already has its own list of suppliers. This means that you will automatically have suppliers that will give the items that you would like for your business. The process that you have to do will be shorter. For example, you just need to choose the product you would like to sell. Then, you are going to chose any of the suppliers that the channel recommends. Lastly, you are just going to wait for the order to arrive.

This may come with some disadvantages, though. Depending on the channel that you will choose to collaborate with, there is a big possibility that you will be disappointed with the service given by the supplier.

Chapter 4: Creating Your Own Website

It has been said that for a supplier to be keen on working with you, you need to prove that your business is ready. What better way to prove that you are ready to do business with them by showing a website that is worthy of checking out? Remember that your website should be impressive enough that it will cause the supplier that you want to approve.

You may think that you are smart by contacting a supplier to do business with you but if you have not set up your own website yet, do not expect suppliers to take you seriously.

Suppliers would also like to deal with drop shipping companies that can protect their brand name and their products. They will not just choose any random company. You need to show them that you have a website that can meet or even exceed their expectations so they would want to work with you.

At this point, you may be thinking that you do not want to waste your time creating your own website when there are other things that you consider more "important" that you need to focus on. It is frustrating because creating a website is not an easy task especially if you do not have any budget to contact a professional to do it for you but remember that without any website, you will not get approved. Even if you try to contact different suppliers, you will still not get approved.

Instead of feeling frustrated because of the need to create your own website, think about this as an experience and investment because the greater your website is, the greater your chances of getting noticed and being picked by suppliers to represent their brand.

Steps to Creating Your Own Website

Having no experience with creating any website before should not stop you from creating one now.

1.   Choose an e-commerce content management system where you want to build your website. This means that you need to find a system that will allow you to customize your website and allow the items that you need.

2.   Most of the website providers that you will see will allow you to pick a theme. There are free themes that are available that can be okay if you are still starting out. After selecting the theme, publish it, so your whole website will follow the theme that you have picked out.

3.   Do some modifications so that your theme will not look like the others. You can make some changes with the font color

depending on the colors of your logo and the colors that you would like to incorporate into your business.

4.   Add the different categories for the different markets that you would like to target through your website. You need to remember that you will be targeting different people in the beginning because you are still starting out. Your items will become more precise as you establish your business but for now, having categories will help. The easier your website is to navigate in, the more customers will check out what you have to offer.

5.   Add your products.

Under the different categories, you can add the products which you think will fit. You cannot put toys under toiletries, right? You need to make sure that they are organized. Depending on the website provide that you will choose this can be easy to do so hard make sure that you will choose wisely.

6.   Add content to your website.

In order to make your website easier to search, you need to make sure that you will add your very own content. Your About Us page is probably the most important. With the proper placement of keywords and as long as you make sure that you will place content that is from the heart, the better.

Convincing Your Supplier through Your Website

Once you have already created a website which you think will wow any supplier, you need to convince them while the website that you created will generate sales.

Remember that suppliers would have to hire new people for the projects that they approve. You need to prove to them while your business will be successful for their business too. They would need to hire a sales representative that will be in charge of explaining to customers (and to you) the products that they offer. They have to provide details and information about all the products that you would like to sell. It will not be easy for suppliers too. This is the reason why they do not approve all of the companies who try to contact them for help.

You Need to Prove That You Can Provide Exceptional Service

A lot of suppliers are wary about hiring random drop shipping companies because they know that they will be affected depending on the service that the company can give. If you can prove to them that your service is always exceptional, then this can be great for their company name too. Remember that it will not be your name that will be affected when people start getting the wrong orders and products. It will be the supplier's name, and they would need to protect their reputation as much as they can in order to be successful in the industry.

Basically, you need to prove to the supplier that you would like to work hand in hand together in order to generate sales. To get approved by a supplier, here are some things you need to remember:

- Make sure that you have some knowledge about e-commerce and you know perfectly well how you are going to market your website if you get approved.

- Continuously study about the different e-commerce techniques that you will use to stand out from a sea of websites available on the Internet and make sure that the supplier that you are trying to work with recognized this.

- You have to be confident in explaining and promoting your website so that the suppliers will also be convinced that partnering with you is also good for their business.

Of course, this is just one of the things that you can do in order to become noticed by a supplier and actually become approved. There are still a lot more that you need to work on but building your own website is the beginning.

CHAPTER THREE

HOW TO PICK THE RIGHT PRODUCTS

The biggest challenge you'll face when you start out as a retailer considering drop shipping is deciding what niche and products to sell. Not surprising, considering that this decision will be the biggest one you make and can make or break your business.

A lot of people make the most basic mistake while deciding. They go for what they are passionate about or are interested in. This is fine if you're more interested in selling a particular product or catering to a particular niche and profits aren't really a concern. But if you want to turn your business into a profitable enterprise, you'll need to do extensive market research on the viability of selling that product or even discard your personal preferences when making such a decision.

Here are some criteria that you'll need to keep in mind when deciding upon your niche and products.

Questions You Need to Ask Before Choosing Any Product

The wide array of products you will see will be enough to confuse you about everything that you could ever need and what you should purchase. You can make it less complicated by asking yourself the following questions:

How much risk am I willing to take?

Do you want to sell high ticket items? Those that are expensive may be harder to sell because of course, not everyone has the money every day to purchase those items. At the same time, the risk may be greater for you if the product would turn out to be defective or problematic. Just remember that if you do decide to take higher priced items, they can also give higher rewards.

Who is my target market?

Who is the market that you are trying to reach? Are you trying to be appealing to the younger market? Perhaps you would like to sell clothing items and accessories that they will find appealing. Once you get to know your target market, it will be easier to make choices about the items that will appeal to them in general.

Are the products easy to search?

The easier the products are to search, the higher the chances that people are searching for those different products online. Of course, if there are a lot of people searching for those items, this is enough reason for you to start selling those items on your website.

How to Sell Online Successfully

If you want your e-commerce business to thrive, you'll need to take one of the following paths.

Manufacturer – If you make your own product and sell it, you are in control of the distribution, and you may be the only source for that product. The advantage here is that you may not face a lot of competition and you can charge a higher price. However, if you want to go the way of drop shipping, this isn't a viable option.

Get Access to Select Distribution or Pricing – One way you can sell online and make a profit without having to manufacture your own product is by having an arrangement with the manufacturer that either lets you exclusively sell the product or gives you access to select pricing. Such arrangements, however, aren't easy to get into. In addition, there are plenty of other drop ship retailers who'll sell similar products and do so at wholesale prices.

Charges the Lowest Price – The most obvious advantage here is that you'll be able to take business away from a lot of your competitors. The reason that it isn't tried very often is that such a business model almost never works. If a low price is all you have to offer to your customers in terms of value, then you'll start a pricing war that will remove pretty much any profit margin you might have. It's not a good idea to compete with online giants such as Amazon based solely on price.

Adds Additional Value by Offering Information – This is the most effective ways to set you apart from the competition and charge a first-rate price. The whole point of entrepreneurship is that you solve problems that people have. This doesn't change when you decide to go the way of drop shipping. If you want your retail enterprise based on drop shipping to work out, the best way to make sure it does is to offer specialist guidance and advice. So the next question that you'll ask is how you can add value.

How to Add Value in E-commerce

Now this is a part that's not quite that easy. There are niches and products in which you can add value quite easily. Then there are others that aren't quite as easy to work with. When trying to do this look for some traits that make it easier for you to add value with content that educates and guides. You need to search for niches and products that:

Have a lot of components – This one is actually quite simple when you think about it. If a product has a lot of components, people are going to go online to figure it out. Buying an office chair is less confusing than buying a DSLR camera with the attendant lenses and other components. It's obvious that if a product needs a lot of components and if those components are quite varied, you have a better chance to add value by letting customers know what products are compatible.

Are confusing or customizable – As Similar to the previous criterion, products that can be customized or require plenty of directions are perfect when you want to add value. If you can offer detailed advice on how certain products fit into different situations, which options are best for them and what product suits what customer, you can add tremendous value.

Need Technical Installation or Setup – Products that are complicated in terms of how they are meant to be installed or set up provide excellent opportunities for you to add value. For example, if you're selling music systems for cars, and you also sell a 40 page guide on how to install the system, what mistakes not to make installing it, how to sync it to your cell phone and so on, people are going to buy the guide from you at the same time as they buy the system to avoid the hassle of having to figure the whole thing out for themselves. Once such guides have been made, you don't have to pay anything to provide them to the customers.

Things You Need to Consider When Deciding Upon the Product

The Best Price – When deciding whether to sell lower or higher-priced products, you will want to consider the level of pre-sale service you can provide. If a customer is going to spend around $150 on a product online, he or she is more likely to buy it without needing to talk to someone on the phone about it. However, if the customer is looking a product priced at $1800, especially one that they don't know much about, they're more likely to want to talk to a sales representative so they can ensure that they're buying something that works for them and that the store is genuine.

If you do decide to go the way of high-priced products, you'll need to ensure two things: that you can provide the level of pre-sale services your customers will expect and that providing such service doesn't eat away into your profit margin. It is a good reason to consider products that range between $100 and $200 since they don't require a lot of pre-sale services.

MAP Pricing – There are manufacturers who set a minimum advertised price (MAP) for the goods they manufacture. In such a case, resellers need to price these products at a specific level or above it, as per the manufacturer. This helps to control price wars that can break out for products that are drop shipped easily. In turn, it also ensures that resellers make a decent profit when they sell that manufacturer's products.

Look for a niche where the manufacturer has enforced MAP pricing. This can be to your advantage, especially if you plan to add value to a site that is high-value and has a wealth of information. Since prices won't be very different from the competition, you won't be competing based on price and instead can compete based on your website, which ensures that you don't lose out to the lower-quality but cheaper competition.

Marketing Potential – You need to plan out your marketing before you begin, not once you've started and then realized that you're having trouble getting customers. Is there a way to promote your store by giving out some products for free or getting in touch with online communities that use the product you sell or even writing articles? If not, then don't consider this niche.

Plenty of Accessories – In general, in the world of retail, margins on higher-priced products aren't nearly as high as those on lower-priced products. For example, although a store that sells televisions may only make a 10% margin on the latest smart TV, it will make a margin of about 100% to 200% on the cables that go with it.

Think about it. When you go to purchase a high-priced item, you're much more careful about how much you end up paying for it. You'll probably shop around for the best smart TV at best possible price. But who shops around for the cables? You don't go from store to store trying to find the best price on something that may cost you about $50 to $60 dollars. You'll probably end up buying it from the store that you bought the TV from.

Low Turnover – By now it should be clear that you will get profits if you go for a good quality site that is rich in information. However, if what you've decided to sell is something that changes or gets updated every year, maintaining such a site will mean a lot of work for you. It is better to invest in products that don't get updated frequently or even every year. This means that the time, money and effort you spend on creating a good site lasts much longer.

Not Easily Available Locally – Your chances of success increase if you're able to identify and sell products that aren't easily available locally but don't get too specific with them. If someone needs a hammer or a garden rake, they're going to check out the neighborhood hardware store. But if you're looking for a falcon training kit or a medieval knight's costume, that isn't so easy. Most people go straight to Google and begin searches.

In Most Cases, Smaller is Better – This is the world of free shipping. Because of this, you may find it difficult to sell large and heavy products that are expensive to ship. Smaller items are easy to ship inexpensively.

While these factors are important, there are two other factors that can trump everything on this list.

Product Demand – Your product may qualify at 100% on the traits I've listed, but you still won't make any money or sell anything if there is no demand for it. You're better off trying to fulfill an existing demand than trying to create a new one. Tools such as Google Keyword Tool and Google Trends can help you identify what the demand for your product is based on search volumes, locations, and search volumes over time, most popular search queries, seasonality and geographic concentration of demand.

Competition – This part can be a bit tricky. If you face too much competition in a particular niche, you could get lost in all the noise out there. However, if you have very little competition, it could mean that there isn't much demand for that niche. While some drop shipping stores do rely on paid advertising, most of them depend on free traffic from search engines. That means that when you research your competition, you need to focus on the sites that come up on the first search page of Google and not the paid ones. When doing this, keep these metrics in mind: a number of linking domains, competing for sites' authority, site usefulness and quality and customer loyalty and site reputation.

Should You Sell Something You Genuinely Like?

There are some people who understand that in order for the items to sell, they need to focus on what the customers want but is this truly the case? Are the customers only the ones that need to be considered? You may want to consider what you want too.

You had started this business because you would like to have the opportunity to build a better future for yourself and probably your family but before you started, what were you doing? Do you consider yourself to be passionate about reading? Perhaps you have always considered decorating to be your strongest skill. You will always have some passions that you can easily incorporate into your business.

When you consider your passion, you find other products to sell that you genuinely want people to see. For example, if you have always loved art but lamented the lack of items that can be used by professionals for their artwork, then you can be the first drop shipping company to find suppliers that can give the type of art products that people are searching for. This will help your site become easier to recognize and appreciate by different individuals.

At the same time, this will allow you to see if there is an opportunity that was not explored yet. When you begin to offer something to the public that they have never seen or experienced before, you will be recognized for it. Even if other drop shipping companies start offering what you are selling, you will have an advantage because you were the first one who started selling it.

A Few More Things to Taking Into Consideration

- If you are going to sell items that have copyright logos, (shirts, books, and other items) you need to make sure that you have gotten the approval of the company that owns the copyright to these products. A case may be filed against you if you are not an authorized seller. It can even be harder if you are selling fakes so try to stay away from counterfeit items.

- Start small with your product selections. It is okay to be passionate about what you are doing and to wish to compete with big brands someday eventually but if you cannot do it yet, then accept this first. The time will come when you will be one of the most successful ones, but as of now, you can practice humility and stay within your range.

- Items that are fragile are always riskier. Let us say that you have always loved ceramics and you know other people who would appreciate if you would sell ceramics as well, but these products come with a higher risk as compared to plastic products that can be sold easily. Consider the pros and cons of each item before deciding if you would offer that item or not.

Top Products Usually Sold in Drop shipping

In case you are still not sure about the variety of products that you are going to sell, here are just a few things that you can add to your line up. Just remember that you are still encouraged to pick depending on your target market.

1.   Beauty Products

You can expect that this is something that people will always need. A lot of women are always on the lookout for beauty products that they can use depending on the occasion. For example, they may need a complete set of eye shadow that will allow them to do a smoky eye makeup. They will purchase different ones available.

2.   Clothing

The thing about clothing is that they are always in demand. As long as you would have the right pieces of clothing to sell, you know that you are going to make a profit. Buyers can purchase a single item, but there are times when they would purchase an entire wardrobe from you. This can do a lot of wonders to your sales.

3. Accessories

Accessories are also other things that are always in demand. As long as you have the right accessories to sell depending on the season, you will be able to sell things and make some profit.

4. Smart Phones

Aside from smart phones, you can sell the usual bar phones if people would want something simple. People are always on the lookout for cell phones that do not cost a lot of money and if you can offer that through your website and you can prove that you will be able to provide good quality smartphones then you have nothing to worry about. The best thing about selling cell phones is that you can sell different ones created by various manufacturers. You are not limited to just one brand so let people explore the options you can offer.

5. Books

Although not everyone can appreciate reading, this is one category that is immensely popular with online shoppers. If you want, you have the option also to sell products that are used. You can search for suppliers that can offer titles that are hard to find and for sure, a lot of bookworms will start checking out your site for the newest titles you can offer.

6.   Toys

This is once again, another category that is always appreciated. There are a lot of kids who would enjoy getting a toy, especially during special occasions. Having a nice selection of toys will allow buyers to purchase from your drop shipping website. Just make sure that you will double check all of the toys that you sell so they are all safe to use.

7.   Furniture

One of the main problems of people, whenever they are purchasing items, is that they have to consider the shipping of the item from the furniture store where they have bought the item. Some people do not like the fact that they have to check the furniture from the actual store and then wait for it to be shipped. Through drop shipping, the item can be picked online, and it will be shipped depending on your rates.

8.   Computer Related Accessories

At this day and age, there are still a lot of people who use computers because it cannot be denied that they are still a strong product that is worth having. You know that you need your computer for your business and there is a big possibility that people use computers for their various purposes as well. Selling accessories that will make computers easier to use can be best sellers.

Other Options

Let us say that you do not want to rely too much on suppliers. What can you do then? If this is the case, the best thing that you can do is to sell your own items. Of course, this takes away the element of drop shipping so if you do this, it will be like you are starting your own online business and you are not starting your very own drop shipping business.

Having the Best Customers

Depending on the products that you are going to sell, you are going to have different customers available. Remember that not all customers are the same. There are some who tend to feel entitled because they have purchased something even if it is just a little trinket and even if the item does not have real value at all.

What you should do is make sure that you will sell the right products so you can attract the right customers to check out your drop shipping company's website. Here are some of the customers that you should attract:

1.   Other businesses - You can expect that business owners are going to buy a lot of items from your website. If you are able to build your relationship with them and eventually get their trust, you know that you will be able to work with them for quite a long time.

2.   Recurring Buyers - You will have some customers who will buy from you often. Whenever they need something, they know that your site is the best option that they have. Having returning customers is always fulfilling because this means that you are slowly building the number of customers who trust your website and your company.

3.   People who have different hobbies - It can be fun to cater to hobbyists because you know that there are always different things that they would like to try and build. You can sell different tools that can cater to various hobbies like woodworking, embroidery, etc.

Measuring the Demand for the Various Products

There should be demand for the items that you are going to sell before they can be sold successfully. For example, if you are going to sell bomber jackets right now, it is guaranteed that you will have more than one customer interested in purchasing because it is in demand. Before you can choose the items that you are going to get from the supplier, you have to know what items are in demand and what items are not in demand. How will you know what is currently in demand?

- Get to know how many people are searching for that particular product. You can check out different keywords that are related to the items. The more keywords are being searched, the bigger the demand for the items/

- Consider the season. You cannot sell Christmas ornaments when Christmas is 11 months away. Of course, you may choose to sell but do you honestly think that people are going to search for Christmas items in the middle of summer? It will be hard to sell swimsuits during winter too unless some people are going to travel to a tropical location.

- Check out the variations that are available. If you try to add some words that are still related to the keywords that you already have and you get good results, then you should delve deeper into those items. It might be worth it in the end.

- Consider the location of people who are searching for the keywords that you are trying to look into. It is true that there are a lot of people who are searching for thigh high boots but these may be people from different continents other than your own. Consider this well so that you can choose.

Now, you may wonder how you can be sure that the niche you've chosen will work out. The answer is that you can't be sure. Everything I've given you in this chapter will increase your chances of success dramatically and help you to pick the right niche. However, certainty will only come once you actually get in and start selling. You will always have doubts before you begin. You're starting a business; the uncertainty is part of that. As long as you merely dream of starting out, you're a dreamer. When you actually do start out and work hard without letting the uncertainty get you down, you become an entrepreneur. Does all the research you need to do and get as much information as you can? But once you've done all of this, don't wait around for the 'perfect market.' There is no such thing. Overcome your fears and get started.

Selling Items You Have Never Seen Before

You need to remember that with drop shipping, you have to sell items direct from suppliers. You are not going to store them somewhere before you sell them. This means that almost if not all items that you are going to sell are things that you have never seen before. How can you sell the right items? Here are some considerations:

Sell Items with Good Reputation - It may be tempting to choose products that seem appealing, but it will not have any sense if they are not quality products that people will not find appealing.

Order some of the Popular Products to Try - In case you would decide later on that these are products that you would not want to keep, you can sell them as "used" items for a lower price. Be specific about the amount of time that you have used the products.

Connect with your Customers from Time to Time - There is a reason why some of your items are selling well while some of your products are not being noticed at all and it is because of what your customers want. Perhaps it will be best if you can talk and connect to your customers. It will make a huge difference.

Checking Out another Drop Shipping Company

Your reason for checking out a drop shipping company may be caused by two reasons. The first reason is you want to scout the competition. You like to see how another drop shipping company deals with various orders. Another reason for trying out a drop shipping company is because you genuinely like to have an item that perhaps you are not selling in your company yet. How will you know if the drop shipping company is legitimate?

- The knowledge of their sales representatives speaks a lot about the company. If their sales representatives can barely say anything when you ask about the items over the phone, you may be dealing with a new business or the sales reps are not trained enough in order to handle answering questions that are supposed to be easy.

- Check their fulfilment speed. You may want to order a few items from them first that do not cost a lot of money before you purchase items from them that will make a dent in your wallet. This will allow you to see how fast they are in fulfilling your orders. At the same time, you can also check if they would communicate with you effectively. There is a need for drop shipping company to communicate with customers so that details regarding shipping and the products that are being sold can be given.

Based on the things that drop shipping companies will do, these are also the things that you have to do with your own drop shipping company if you would decide to push through with this.

CHAPTER FOUR

HOW TO START YOUR BUSINESS

By this time, you should be very familiar with the basics of drop shipping. You may have started thinking about starting your own retail business. If you are truly serious about becoming an entrepreneur, you'll need to take the following steps in terms of finance and business. While some of the steps are necessary to set up a business, others are merely good ideas that help in the long run. Deal with all these steps now so you have fewer challenges down the road.

Choosing the Perfect Business Name

You already know the things that you are going to do, and you have even formulated your own website, but you have to admit that you did not focus on choosing the right business name that will be helpful for your business.

Choosing the right business name does not have a clear formula that will give the results that you have always wanted but at least, with proper knowledge, it will be easier for you to formulate a business name that people will take seriously. You will have a business name that people will recognize so you will have a drop shipping company that people would like to buy from.

Here are some tips:

1.   Do not be in haste when making a choice.

One of the most common mistakes that people make when it comes to choosing the right drop shipping business name is they choose the very first one that they see. Remember that thinking of a business name will require a bit of time. Although it will not take up all of your time, your brand name is crucial for your business.

Remember that your business name is something that people will remember forever. If people would have good or bad experiences with dealing with you (but hopefully all good,) they will remember those experiences. It can improve the number of people who would shop from your website.

When you rush, you may choose a name that is highly limiting. For example, if you would choose a company name that is only connected to lights because these are the items that you initially sell, it will be harder for your other products to be recognized when you start selling other items that are not related to lights at all.

2.   It is okay to consider what you want, what your family wants and what your friends would like but you have to consider your audience and what will lure them to check out what you have to offer.

The business name that you are going to pick should be in close connection with the audience that you are trying to please, the people that you are trying to target. It is normal for your family and friends to be supportive by giving what they think will be awesome for your drop shipping company but unless they represent a large percentage of your target market, their ideas might be bad for your business.

One of the best choices that you can make in order to know what your customers want is to create a survey. There are some websites that will allow you to do random surveys that can be answered by people who are just browsing. There are also some paid surveys that will give more accurate results. It will depend on you and what you think is best for your company.

Another thing that you can do is to conduct your own research. Since it is likely that you have not opened your company to the public yet because you still do not have a business name, you can always research about the usual keywords that your target market search for. You can incorporate some of those keywords into your brand name so that it will be appealing to them.

3.   **You should keep your business name short.**

You may be tempted to have a long and complicated business name that has never been used before, but there may be a reason why it was never used. It may be because it is too long. Most business names do not exceed 15 characters because if you make your business name longer than that, people will become confused.

Another thing to remember is that your business name should be easy to spell. How will people search for something when the spelling isn't correct? This may be bad for your business later on. You may think that the best thing to do in order to become recognizable is to think of a business that is sort of like a pun. It might be fun in the beginning, but it might become a joke later on. Besides, if you do this, people will not be taking your business very seriously.

4.   **Do not have a business name depending on what you do.**

It might be easy to name your business isellbooks.com if you plan on selling books perhaps you may even want your URL to be youlightupmylife.com because generally, you sell lights, but your business name does not have to reflect that. Your business name should be formal and easy to pronounce.

5. Try to think of a name that will appeal to different parts of the globe.

It is true that since you are starting your drop shipping company, you are only targeting the local market but this does not mean that you will never have a chance to sell to the rest of the world someday. When you think of a limiting name, it might become a joke to your future customers, and of course, you cannot change your company name when you are already successful as it might be confusing to the consumers.

The Process to Follow in Creating a Business Name

You should have a business name that will be appealing to your target audience but how you are going to find out what appeals to them? Here are some steps that will help you do just that:

1. Find out the keywords that your target audience usually use. Pick some of the keywords that you think will sound great when added to your business name.

2. Create a list that holds a lot of the potential names that you have come up so far. It is okay in the beginning to have so many business names because of course, you are still trying to choose the one that is perfect for you.

3.   Consider the tips that are mentioned above. It is likely that you are going to eliminate a lot of business names because of the tips.

4.   Create a survey that can be answered by your target audience. Once again, this will depend on you if you would like the service to be given out by a free website or a paid one. A paid website will give more accurate results, but if you do not have enough budgets for that, the free website can be enough.

In case you do not have people to ask the survey to just yet, you may create a social media page that can be shared by different people. The more people from your target market answer, the better your results are going to be.

5. The moment that you have already chosen the right name for your business, you need to make sure that it is not used by another business. At the same time, you would not want other businesses to imitate your business name so have it registered and make sure that it is legal.

Commitment

Building a business using drop shipping is essentially the same as building any other business. You need to put in all the commitment possible and think long-term. Don't be seduced by online claims. You're not going to earn a six-figure income doing part time work for six weeks. Be realistic about how much investment you need to put in, how much profitability you can expect, and it will ensure that you don't lose heart at the first few obstacles and give up.

You either need to invest a lot of time or a lot of money when you set up a business based on drop shipping.

Time

If this is the first time you're getting into the field of drop shipping or even if this isn't your first rodeo, you are better off investing sweat equity and bootstrapping. There are many reasons this is a better approach than investing a huge amount of capital:

- This is the best way to know your business completely from the basics to the complexities involved – something that becomes vital once your business grows and you need to manage others.

- You can make better decisions because you'll know your market and customers intimately.

- There is less chance that you'll invest huge amounts of money into vanity projects that aren't going to matter much in the long-run.

- You'll acquire and develop many skills, all of which make you a better businessperson.

Let's be real. You're not going to quit your job to spend the next three or six or even nine months building up an online store. It is a better idea to start doing this while still in your 9 to 5 routine. Of course, it's going to be difficult, and you'll need to make sure those proper expectations regarding fulfillment times and customer service for your customers is set. Once your business scales and grows, you can move into taking care of your business full-time, depending on profitability and cash flow.

While each entrepreneur and business are different, you can start making between $1000 and $2000 a month within 12 months by spending around 10 to 15 hours every week to build your business.

Of course, if operating your business full-time right from the start is viable, then there is nothing like it. It is a good idea to focus your effort on promotion and marketing, especially early on when momentum is vital to the success of your business.

Now all of this may seem like you're putting in a lot of effort for returns that aren't very inspiring. However, think about these two things:

- Once you've gotten your online store that is based on drop shipping off the ground, running the store is going to take much less time than the regular 4o hour week. What you've invested initially gives you good returns in terms of the scalability and efficiency that the drop shipping model offers.

- This isn't just a business that earns you income. This is an asset that you can sell in the future. When you're looking at true returns, don't just focus on the cash flow. Consider the equity value as well.

Money

You can build a business based on drop shipping by investing huge amounts of capital. However, when it comes to outsourcing the business versus building it yourself, you'll find that you achieve the most success by taking care of the business by yourself.

It becomes absolutely critical that in the early stages of the business, you have someone who is very deeply invested in its success and builds it from scratch. If you don't have an in-depth understanding of every step of how your business works, you'll soon find that your profits are eaten up by expensive marketers, developers, and programmers. While you don't have to do absolutely everything yourself, it is a good idea to be the one behind the business instead of paying someone else to do it.

This doesn't mean that you can get started without any financial investment whatsoever. When you start out, you'll need to have at least $1000 to get your business off the ground. This money is generally used for operating expenses such as suppliers and web hosting and to pay any fees involved in incorporating your business.

Determining the Business Structure to Use

The first thing I want to mention here is that the information about business structures I discuss in this book is valid in the United States, not in other countries.

The first thing you'll need to do when you decide to launch your project is to set up a business entity that is legal and legitimate. For detailed legal advice, it is best to contact a lawyer, but here is an overview of the three most common business structures.

Sole Proprietorship – While this business structure is the simplest to execute, there is no personal liability protection here. This means that if your business is sued, your personal assets may go as well. There aren't too many filing requirements, and all you have to do is report the earnings from your business when doing your personal taxes. Federal or state business filings apart from this aren't needed.

Limited Liability Corporation (LLC) – When it comes to an LLC, your business is established as a separate legal entity, which means that your personal assets are protected. This doesn't give you a foolproof liability protection but is significantly better than a sole proprietorship. There will be more filing requirements involved and you'll also have to pay ongoing fees as well as an incorporation fee.

C Corporation – Most of the larger corporations are set up this way. This is because when this is done right, it offers you the most liability protection. Incorporating this is more expensive, and you can expect double the taxes since the income doesn't go directly to the shareholders.

If you want to know which structure to choose from these, I recommend that you talk to a lawyer in detail before deciding. Smaller entrepreneurs tend to go with LLCs or sole proprietorships.

Requesting an EIN

As per the IRS, all businesses need to have an EIN or employer identification number. This is basically your business' social security number. This is the number you need to apply for a drop shipping account with a wholesaler, file your taxes, start a bank account for your business and perform all other such transactions that have to do with your business.

You can get an EIN for free online.

Arrange Your Finances

A very common mistake made by most entrepreneurs in the field of drop shipping is merging business and personal finances. First of all, this becomes confusing. Secondly, your accounting will be a mess. Thirdly, you'll have to take the personal assumption of business liabilities which means that your personal assets are on the line every time you're sued. Lastly and most importantly, if you're audited by the IRS, this is considered a huge red flag.

It is very important to separate your personal and business finances. It is best that you open a separate account that is in your business' name. Here are the accounts that you'll need to open.

Business Checking Account – It is most advisable to operate your business finances' through a primary checking account. This is where you deposit all your business revenues and from where you withdraw all your business' expenses. Your accounting will be much more straightforward and easy after you do this.

PayPal Account – If like most online retailers, you plan to accept PayPal, you will need to create a separate account as a business.

Credit Card – It is best if you have a credit card in the name of your business that you use solely to pay business expenditures and to purchase inventory through drop shipping. Remember what I said earlier about rewards? Since this is how you'll be paying the suppliers, you will end up with a lot of reward points or cash back or even frequent flyer miles. Shop around and see what credit cards offer the right rewards.

Collect Sales Tax

The only time you need to collect sales tax is when

- The state in which you operate collects sales tax AND

- Someone living in your state places an order

When residents from other states place orders, you don't need to collect sales tax from them, even if their own state does charge. Remember that as of now, the small time online entrepreneurs have advantages in terms of taxes. Don't rely too heavily on them as they may be changed in the years to come.

If the state that you operate in does charge a sales tax, you need to be ready to collect it from the customers who are also in your state and who order something from you. Get in touch with the Department of Commerce in your state and register as a retail business. Then find out how often you must submit the collected sales tax.

Local Business Licenses

In most towns and cities in the United States, you need to get a business license to operate a business. This license will need to be renewed every year. It means that there may be no such requirements when it comes to such businesses that rely on drop shipping. This is because such businesses are usually small operations that are run out of home offices. Check your local regulations to see what your town's or city's stance is on this.

Incorporating Outside the U.S.

While it is not the purpose of the book to guide you in detail about how to incorporate if you're based outside the U.S., I will give you some information. You can incorporate a business in the United States, which will give you access to U.S. customers and drop shippers. However, there is always paperwork to be done to incorporate, and you will need to come to the U.S. to do this. Alternatively, you can trust a business partner in the U.S. who will take care of everything stateside and act on your behalf, or you can hire an agency.

CHAPTER FIVE

WHAT CHANNELS SHOULD YOU SELL THROUGH?

You've picked your product and niche, determined who your suppliers are going to be and established your business legally. Now it's time to sell! Your next decision has to be how to get the products in front of your customers. There are plenty of options to choose from. However, the most likely options you'll choose are to sell on eBay, Amazon or your own online store.

Drop shipping on eBay

eBay is quite possibly the world's largest online auction site where you can buy and sell physical goods, and most people are familiar with it. Here are some pros and cons of launching your retail business through eBay.

Pros

Start Easily – On eBay, all you have to do is create an account, begin a listing and your business is up and running.

Extensive Audience – Listing on eBay gives you access to millions of people who use this giant. A lot of people are going to see your listings. Also, the market is active and healthy so you can get a fairly good price for your products.

Less Marketing – When you list on eBay, you don't have to concern yourself with SEO, paying for traffic or marketing. You're basically piggybacking off eBay's platform which is gigantic. Since one of the biggest tests of launching a business based on drop shipping is marketing, you end up saving a lot of time.

Cons

Listing Fees – This is one of the biggest cons of using eBay. There are a lot of fees that you need to pay for the platform, one of the biggest of which is the success fees. The success fee can be 10% or more of your products' sales price. The profit margins in the drop shipping market are already fairly thin, so this can eat into your revenue.

Regular Re-listing and Monitoring – Since eBay is an auction market, you will need to re-list and monitor your products on a frequent and regular basis. While eBay does have tools that can automate this process to an extent, it is much more straightforward to list a fixed product for sale on your own website.

Sales Platform Not Customizable – Since eBay has specific templates that you need to follow, you can't create a page that is professional and adds value for your customers.

No Long-term Customer Relationships – Most eBay customers will only buy from you once. While some customers may return, providing good service will not give you any dividends in terms of return traffic. Since the focus is on the product and not the merchant, you will face restrictions in terms of how you interact with your customers, your store design, and your branding and other features.

Drop Shipping on Amazon

Amazon does stock products and sells them. However, a lot of products up for sale on the site are sold by third-party retailers via the Amazon website. Amazon helps with the sale and any problems that may arise.

Pros

The pros here are much the same as those that you have in going via eBay – a large audience, easy to begin and no need for SEO and marketing. In addition, Amazon has its own warehouses known as Fulfillment by Amazon. These warehouses permit you to sell your own products on the site without having to worry about shipping, packing or storage.

Cons

The cons here are pretty much the same as eBay – commission fees that eat into your profits, no customization and no long term connection with customers. In addition, all your sales data is available to Amazon. The online giant has been accused of using this information to figure out the good selling items and to reinforce its own position, thereby pushing other retailers out of its marketplace.

Drop Shipping With Your Own Store Online

If you don't want to go through avenues such as eBay and Amazon, an alternative is to start your own online store from where you can sell. Most people who want to build a successful online retail operation through drop shipping tend to use this method.

Pros

Control – You have full control here in terms of creating a site that leans toward selling your products and on which you can add value for your customers. The look, layout, and experience are customizable allowing you to educate your customers about the products you sell in the best possible way.

Easy Design – It is quite easy to build your own online store. There are plenty of platforms such as Shopify that can help you with this. All you need to do is select a store design (you have hundreds of choices), customize the design however you desire, add the products you're going to sell and set up a payment gateway. It can even be done in one day, depending on what type of store you want to set up.

No Fees to Third-parties – There are no commissions you need to pay that eat into your profit margin.

Building an Asset – Your business will be long-term, unique and will have repeat customers. In doing this, you will build up a business which has equity. You will find it a lot easier to sell a business that has been set up around a website.

Cons

Less Free Traffic – When you create your own website, you are the one responsible for directing traffic to it. This means that marketing, paid advertising, and SEO are things that you'll need to take care of. As such, you'll pay more here and need to conduct long-term operations to promote your site.

More Complex – eBay and Amazon offer you standard templates which you use to create a listing. When it comes to your own store, things aren't quite as simple. You have to decide the layout, design, and structure. If you're hosting your own store, you'll need to take care of technical aspects such as servers and software.

So What Should You Choose?

That really depends on what you want to do. If you want to do this as a way to earn some extra income on the side or as a hobby, then Amazon and eBay are your best bets to getting started. You'll need to find products that give you plenty of margins that you can pay the fees and still earn a profit. People are making money via these platforms so don't ignore them.

However, if you want to venture into retail and set up your own business, the best thing to do is launch your own online store. As I've mentioned above, doing so has advantages in terms of customizability, customer connection, and building brand equity. Going this way has a lot of long-term potentials.

Considering Multi Channel Selling

You may be trying to contemplate on which one you are going to choose that you have already spent a lot of time trying to consider each of the channels mentioned above. Why should you choose just one channel when you can sell in all of them?

What is Multi Channel Selling?

From the name itself, you can already guess that multi-channel selling pertains to selling your items in different channels available. This includes selling items from your own website as well.

According to results, those who try multi-channel selling end up having more sales than those who sell in only one channel. This is because you increase your chances of being seen by different individuals. For example, there are some people who only check out eBay but do not check out Amazon and vice versa. By selling through those different channels, you are reaching out to more people. You are improving and increasing your market in the process as well.

At this point in time, your main issue may be how you are going to place all of the inventory data in these different channels. Admittedly, manually inputting the data can take a long period of time. There is a big possibility that after placing all of the data in one channel, you do not want to do it again with another channel afterwards.

The best solution to this is to find inventory management software. You may be thinking that this will just add up to your many expenses but consider the sales that you are going to generate because of multi channel selling; it will be worth it in the end. If you want to be more careful, you can always start by selling in just one channel, and as you try to expand your business further, that is the time when you can invest in the software and try selling from different channels that are available to you.

The Process to Follow

Let us say that you have decided to do multi channel selling, but you do not know where to begin. Here is the process that will make things easier for you:

1.   Make sure that you have accounts on all the channels that you wish to sell from. How can you sell from Amazon when you do not even have an account? Open an account and make sure that you will clearly input your business name there as this will create a lot of difference.

2.   Start uploading your product data. You know that this can take a long time, but with the help of the right software, it will be a breeze. You can just double check the data once you have uploaded everything to be sure that are satisfied with how all of the items have been uploaded.

3.   You can wait for the orders to start to arrive. It is highly likely that the orders will arrive soon because you are able to reach more people. There will be different orders that you will get, make sure that you fulfil them all. Follow the standard process, so you will not be confused.

CHAPTER SIX

HOW TO COMPETE WITH OTHER DROP SHIPPING COMPANIES

One of the problems that you are going to have when you start your own drop shipping company is the fact that you have to compete with a lot of other drop shipping companies that may be located in the same area. If you have too much competition from where you are located, it will be harder for you to be noticed especially if your competitors are already well known and have already established their reputation.

You can always opt to rely on free traffic. You would rely on how well your website has been created so that people can visit your site whenever they try to search for the use of a search engine. Yet, this can still be complicated. In order to stand out, you need to generate a good amount of traffic, and you can do this by using paid advertising.

You have to rely on your website in order to be noticed heavily and for people to come back and check the items that you are offering. Let us focus first on your website's content. Here are just some of the things that you can add:

- Consider the number of linking domains - The more links that you will have on your website, the better your website's ranking is going to be. Remember that duplicate links will not be considered by search engine sites, so they will not be effective at all.

- Consider the quality of your website. It does not mean that just because you have a lot of links, your website will already be one of the websites that will rank high in search engine sites. The quality of your content and how relevant the content will be will make a huge difference. You can compare the current quality of your website with the others with the use of different applications. Your page rank can be easily checked when you have the right tools, but in case you would like to check manually, this is possible as well.

It is evident that if you would be one of the first few websites that will appear in search engine sites; you will be checked out by more people. In case you do not understand the page ranking, here is a guide that will let you understand the differences of each:

Page Rank 1 - 2: You have a small amount of authority. This means that you are able to reach a small amount of your target market.

Page Rank 3- 4: This is the common page rank of websites that are competing well with other websites. If you get this page rank, this means that you have a high sense of authority and will be displayed in one of the first few pages of search engine sites.

Page Rank 4- 5: There are some websites who do not get to this point anymore because the website needs to be connected to other websites that are also considered to have high page ranks. To reach this rank, you need your website to be linked to different websites.

Page Rank 6+: It will be hard to compete in this type of page rank. You need to employ a full time SEO expert that will be able to let your website keep up with the changing times. At the same time, you need to make sure that your marketing is always in full gear. If you do not have professionals working for you, you will be lost in this type of page rank.

Deciphering Your Page Results

Do you realize that the page results that you get are different from other people in different countries who are searching for the same things that you have typed in the search bar? This is because search engine sites make it a point to consider your geographic location. This makes searching for the right items to sell easier because you are looking at what other people within the same location are interested in.

Aside from your current location, search engine sites also consider your browsing history. This can again alter your results from another person in the same location that are searching for the same keywords you have typed in. If you want to truly see the page results without other factors altering the results you are going to get, there are a few things that you can do:

1.   Aside from your usual keyword, you can add a location that will make the results more specific towards the location that you are interested in checking out. This is very easy to do and can already give you the result that you want.

2.   Try searching in incognito mode. This will give you an unbiased ranking of the website. It will not be based on how many times you have checked that same website in the past. You will see if the keywords that you have typed in are truly relevant or not.

How to Let Customers Stay at Your Website

Even if you were able to configure your website so that it will be one of the websites that will appear first when people start searching, the ranking would not guarantee that they will continue to navigate your website and actually purchase from you. What do you think should you do in order to let customers stay? You need to work on your website appropriately.

- Make sure that your website has an appealing design - It will help if the design of your website is something that people find nice to look at. If they think that your website looks dirty and if the different links are all over the place, then it will not be very pleasing.

- The design that you are going to pick out should be connected to drop shipping - It does not necessarily have to have the word drop shipping all over the website but rather, your website should look like a drop shipping site with a twist.

- The navigation should be easy - If people do not understand how to get from one page to another, then you can already expect that navigation will not be very easy to do and you will lose potential customers in the process.

- Get rid of ads that cover the whole page - One of the things that can turn off a lot of people into visiting various websites is having an advertisement flashed on the screen. If this is something that you never liked in other websites before then why should you do it to yours?

- Let customers browse through your website before giving them an option to register so that they can start purchasing from your website. Remember that when you force people to register for your website, you can expect that they will rather not go through with it.

- Add videos and images - Do not underestimate the power of videos and images on your website. Each item that you are selling should have images because you want people to see how the items look like. Just be specific if you think that the item may not look exactly the same with how it looks like in pictures. Videos can be endearing for some and can let them stay for more than a few minutes.

- Let them find what they need - You may want to put a lot of fluff, but it would be similar to having a useless PowerPoint presentation with a lot of animation. You do not need to let your website become animated to become noticed. They have checked your website in the first place in order to look at your items. Let them see what items you are selling. It will make a huge difference with how long they will stay.

- Do not have a laggy site - Do you know one of the reasons why people decide to navigate away from a website? It is because the website is not responding properly to the actions that they want. For example, if they click on an item with the use of their mouse button, it takes more than 10 seconds before the image becomes big enough for them to see. When your website is laggy, they would rather search elsewhere.

- If you have links, make sure that they are easy to find - There may be some links that they can click on in order to get to another portion of your website. Make these links visible.

- Have a page on your website that talks about the frequently asked questions regarding your website, what you offer and the things that you sell. Remember that no matter how nice you thought you had created your website, there are some customers who will not understand a few things. As long as you place some FAQ, your customers will know that you are trying your best to address their current issues.

Figuring Out the Rest

At this point in time, you already know how you can compete with competitors so that people will start checking out your website too but how will you know if the strategies that you are planning will actually work? You will never know if it is going to work or not. There are some people who were able to implement changes to their website at the right time, so they become more established easier but there are also some who may have to struggle for months before they become noticed by customers.

A FEW COMMON PROBLEMS EXPERIENCED WITH DROP SHIPPING

You have to understand that even with all of the things that are mentioned above, drop shipping is not easy. It is not exactly one of the things that you can do if you want to make a lot of money at the soonest possible time. The things that will be discussed below are common issues that you have to consider before you start the company but don't worry. As long as you are determined and as long as you know how to plan appropriately, these problems can be resolved easily.

1.   **Out of stock items when customers want the same product**.

The best solution to this is to make sure that you will be working with more than one supplier that can offer similar products. It is likely that some of these products are so similar that people will not notice that they are different from one another.

2.   Syncing products can be tedious and will take time.

Since you do not have all day to just properly synchronize your database about all of the products that you are offering to clients, the best solution is to have the right application or software that can do the synchronization for you. You can simply add or remove items depending on whether you would like to sell them or not.

3.   You will be selling items that you will never see.

It is true that as a drop shipper, the items that you are selling to customers are items that you will never see in person. This means that it will be harder to know if the item is really worth it or not. You can just base it on the pictures which you know, may not be too accurate.

In order to solve this problem, you can always call the supplier that you are going to get the products from to ask some questions about the product in general. In case this is not enough, why not purchase some of your most popular products and get to know their different features. You may understand why they are so popular and why you always run out of these items.

4.   You cannot control customer service.

Aside from the reputation of your company, another thing that is important is the customer service that you can provide. As a drop shipping company, you have no control over the type of service that your customers will get.

The perfect solution to this is to try your best to choose the right people who will help you and your business thrive well in this type of industry. If you feel that the people you are currently working with are doing nothing to help you give the customer service that your customers deserve, search for other people to partner with.

The Problems Your Customers Would Like to Avoid

A lot of customers know that purchasing from a drop shipping company is a great way for customers to get to see different products without having to go from one website to another. Customers know that there are also some cons when it comes to dropping shipping and they would like to avoid it. Here are a few common problems and how you can make sure that your customers will not experience those problems.

1.   Poor Details Regarding Orders

Whenever customers order from your drop shipping company, they would like to make sure that they will get their products immediately. In order not to disappoint your customers regarding their orders, you can send them their tracking number so that they can check the status of their orders from your website. Of course, in order to sync all of the orders, make sure that you will talk with your suppliers regarding when the items will be shipped. It will also help if you can contact the customers regarding their orders and be specific about when their orders are expected to arrive.

2.   Their Orders are not what They Expected

As an owner of a drop shipping company, you have never seen in person most of the items that you are selling. You can only base the items from the description that the suppliers give. This is the reason why there are some customers who may complain about the appearance of the items that they have received. The best thing that you can do about this is to double check the products that you are going to offer on your website ahead of time. You can contact the supplier and do not hesitate to ask questions, so you will have a clear view of the items before you let them become available through your website.

3.   The items they will get are damaged.

It can be very frustrating for a customer to get damaged items because the main reason why they have purchased from your company is so they can avoid rushing with the crowd. In case the item that gets shipped to the customer is damaged, you can please your customer by replacing the item without having to let the customer send back the damaged item. This action can win a lot of points for your drop shipping company.

CHAPTER EIGHT

HOW TO RUN YOUR DROP SHIPPING COMPANY

You have already heard earlier about how you can start your business, but you have no idea about what you should do in order to run it. Studying about how to run your very own drop shipping company can save you some weeks and months of being frustrated.

Things Are Bound to Getting Messy - Since drop shipping is considered convenient, you can expect that it can be confusing as each sale can be complicated especially when other parties are involved. There will be botched orders at times. Some items will be out of stock. You may not be able to fulfil all of the duties you are required to do.

Keep it Simple - You already know that drop shipping is very complicated. You do not have to complicate it further by messing up your system. Make sure that you have created a flawless system that you will follow so that you can track down your inventory and the costs that you have to pay for every time. Instead of choosing some complicated methods, you can choose simpler methods that will do the job well.

Making Things Run Smoothly

The two things that are mentioned above are tips that will help keep you sane while running a drop shipping company. You have to be prepared to run things smoothly depending on the situations that you will encounter. Here are just a few of the possible issues:

- Your Supplier has Botched an Order

Even if you already trust your supplier, there will be times when they will make mistakes and you now owning up to the mistake can make things worse. Here are just a few of the things that you can do:

- You may want to offer something else to the customer for free in order to make up for the error. It is the best way that you can smooth out the problem.

- Apologize to the customer for the mistake. If your customer is not aware that you have a drop shipper, it will only be confusing for the customer. Do not act like an amateur. Admit the mistake and do what you can to pacify the customer.

- Allow the supplier to pay for the mistake. Even though you have apologized to the customer for the mistake, it is still not your mistake. If you are dealing with a professional shipping company, they know that they have to pay for the error.

If the supplier where you normally get your items from botch up orders regularly, it is time to search for a new supplier. There are other suppliers who can offer better services than the one you are experiencing.

You have Trouble Managing Your Items

It is only common that you will have some issues with managing your items especially if you have not formulated the right system to follow. If you do a poor job, you may tell some customers that some of your items are available when they are actually out of stock. The constant mistake will turn a lot of customers off. You will lose a lot of customers in the process.

In order to manage your inventory, here are a few things that you can do:

1.   Make sure that you have an application that will allow you to keep track of your items easily. We do not live in the Stone Age anymore. You now have a lot of options to make the management of your items easier. Make use of these applications

and tools and keeping track of the various items from suppliers will be easier.

2.   Have separate files for each supplier. It is only common that you are going to have more than one supplier in order to provide the different items that you need to sell. If you only have one supplier, then you will not have anything to sell if the supplier fails to submit the items you need.

Having more than one supplier can be complicated, though. You may keep track of all the items that you get from one supplier and separate that from the items you get from another supplier. This will allow you to check and see which items are truly out of stock and which ones you still have a lot of.

3.   Do not just pick all of the products that suppliers are offering. It may be tempting to pick out all of the cute products that you see. It can also be easy just to choose products that seem to fit your business, but you also have to remember the quality of the items. Are the items worth purchasing? Will people actually pay a lot of money for the items that you are choosing? If you are unsure with which products of picking, choose primary items that are known to sell well.

4.   It is okay to pick similar items from different suppliers as long as they look identical. This way, even if the items from one

supplier run out, you will have a similar one ready that you can sell to your potential customers.

5.   Always coordinate with your sales representative. Your sales representative is here for a reason, and that is to make sure that you will be getting items that will improve your company's name and branding. Always check if the items are available and inform your representative when to start purchasing again, so you will not run out of supplies.

In case even if you have tried your best to manage your stocks you still run out of certain items, tell your customer about it and offer another item that may appease your customer. If the item you are selling appeals to the customer, then you have nothing to worry about. It will even improve your relationship with the customer.

You Have Hired a Bad Vendor

A lot of the items that you are selling will be reliant on your vendor. When a vendor is bad, you will lose time in order to do other things because you will do nothing but follow up the orders of the customers and when they will be shipped. When you have a bad vendor, you can expect that your customers will be irate with you because they were not able to get their items on time. You may even lose customers in the process because they feel like you are wasting their time. At the same time, you know that by hiring the wrong vendor, you are wasting your time and money too.

Not all vendors are good so before you choose a vendor that will be your partner in your business, make sure that you will select a vendor who has already built up a good reputation. To make choosing vendors easier, you can base it on the following:

- Have criteria that you would like to follow when searching for the right vendor. If one criterion are not achieved by the vendor, then search for another one that can fit your needs better.

- Make sure that you will set up a written document wherein your vendor will have to agree with the different terms and conditions that will allow your business to operate smoothly. The document that you are going to create with the help of the lawyer may outline shipping times, inventory updates, order exception resolution among others. This will let you and your vendor know what to do to have a good relationship and work together properly.

- If you have more than one vendor, create your very own vendor scorecard, so you will know at the end of the year who among the vendors you are going to keep and who the ones that you will part ways with are. You only need to do what is best for your business.

When you have a bad vendor, you can cut ties with the vendor unless you have a contract that you have to follow. The moment that you are legally allowed to search for a new vendor do it for the improvement of your drop shipping business.

Dealing with Security and Issues on Fraud

Credit Card Information Storing

If you are going to host your own site, you have to be aware of the following:

- Get to know the Payment Card Industry (PCI) rules. You have to be aware that this is going to cost a lot of money. There are a lot of compliance rules and audit that you have to be aware of.

- In case your client gets his/her account information hacked, it will be your responsibility.

Knowing that it can be complicated, it is sometimes best if you are only starting your company, that you will not store the credit card information of your clients. You can start venturing into it once your business becomes bigger, but as of now, there are other options that are available that will not make handling your business more complicated than it already is.

Verification System

Since you are only starting out, it is okay to be intimidated with dealing orders and making sure that they are all correct. Remember that you need common sense and caution all the time.

Getting to Know the Address Verification System

In order to prevent fraud, using the Address Verification System will surely help. This requires customers to enter their address connected to their credit card in order to become approved. Through this, credit card thieves will be prevented from making purchases because most of them do not know where the listed addresses are of the credit cards they have stolen. It is already rare for fraud orders to pass through with this system.

It is evident that the order may be considered fraudulent when the billing address and the shipping address are different. If you do not allow items to be released when the billing address and the shipping address is different, however, you will lose sales if you would not allow this to occur so what the signs that you should watch out for in order to know if the order is fraudulent or not are?

- The names are different - The names may be different because of two possible reasons. The first reason is that the order is fraudulent while the second reason is that the purchase is a gift.

- E-mail addresses do not seem authentic - It is very easy to create a free e-mail address but normally, people who use their e-mail address will incorporate a part of their name into it. If you see e-mail addresses that make no sense, this may be a sign of fraud.

- Most expensive shipping - Since a lot of fraudsters are paying with another person's credit card; they do not care if they pick the most expensive way to ship. Of course, this can also mean that they would like to get the items that they ordered immediately.

So what should you do if you suspect that an order is a fraud? This is the time when you should make good use of your phone. Remember that since a lot of people would not like to put their real numbers on their order, you will either get a false number or you can get the number where you can talk to the person who ordered, so everything will be cleared. Honestly, this is easy to do in the beginning when you are not getting enough orders yet but can be more complicated and harder to monitor when you are handling a lot of orders at the same time.

Chargeback's

Do you understand what chargeback is? Basically, this is when a customer contacts his/her credit card company to complain about a charge that your company has made. The amount will temporarily be taken from your account, and you have to prove that you were able to provide the services or items to the customer who has complained of getting charged. It is okay if you can find proof but if you don't, there will be a processing fee charged to your account. The worst thing that can happen is you will not be given the privilege of having a merchant account anymore.

There are different reasons for getting chargebacks:

- Fraud

- The customer forgot about ordering

- The customer did not like the item or service received.

When you receive a chargeback, it is not the proper time to contemplate about what have gone wrong. You barely have time to do anything so make sure that you will do your best to answer as quickly as you can.

To Get Your Money Back

You have been charged a certain fee because of the chargeback, and your main goal is to get your money back. How are you going to do that? Remember to provide documentation which proves that you have delivered the items ordered from you. If the transaction is legitimate, your chances of getting your money back are certain.

To Win the Issue

You need the billing and the shipping address on the card information details to be the same. If the details are not the same, your chances of getting a charge back lessen.

Dealing with Returns

It may be easy to start making your own return policy without realizing how other suppliers do it. You have to understand the policy of each supplier that you have. It will make dealing with things easier. For example, they may have a 60 day return policy. When this occurs, you can be generous with your return policy as well. Of course, if you have more than one supplier, you have to consider all so even if there is one that offers 60 day return policy, if the other one only offers 45 day return policy, you need to adjust your terms.

How Customers Return Items

This is the process followed by customers whenever they need to return items:

1.   A customer requests to return the item/s received.

2.   You talk to your supplier about getting a Return Merchandise Authorization.

3.   The customer mails the item back to the supplier and not to you. Take note of this. The RMA# should be specified.

4.   The supplier refunds the amount.

5.   You return the funds to your customer in full amount.

The process seems to be easy right? Yet, if you have tried returning an item that you do not like in the past, you know that there are different things that can complicate the return process.

Defective Items

When it comes to defective items, you are risking your business because people might not want to order from you again because you are selling something that does not work. Another bad thing about this is that you would have to pay for shipping. Unfortunately, you cannot pass on this fee to anyone else.

If the item is inexpensive, it may be a better option to let the customer keep the old item and just ship a new one, but if it is expensive, then you may have to ask the customer to return it while you handle the shipping fees.

Here are some of the advantages that can be received if the items are simply exchanged without the need for the defective items to be shipped back:

- It is more cost effective - It may not be worth it to spend a lot of money on shipping the defective item back to you if the shipping is worth the actual cost of the item.

- You will score major points with the client - It is very rare that companies will allow clients not to return the old item anymore so if you do this, you can expect that your clients will be blown away and would be more trusting when it comes to dealing with you.

- You may talk your supplier into handling the shipping costs of the new items that will be sent to the client. This will depend on your relationship with your supplier, though.

A lot of companies usually require the buyers to handle the shipping fee of returning various items that they have ordered, even if the item is defective. In order to stand out, you can order free shipping. You can expect that customers will take note of this.

A Few Possible Issues with Shipping Rates

When it comes to shipping rates, it can be very complicated if you have more than one supplier. Once again, you need to adjust your rates depending on the costs. To make the rates more uniform and less complicated, here are some ideas:

- Type Rates - This means that you are going to have rates depending on the type of items that are being ordered by the client.

- Flat Rate - This may be the easiest one. There will be a standard flat rate that will be followed no matter what the items that are ordered are.

- Real Time Rates - You will have to compute the real amount of shipping based on the items that are ordered and the client's location. It can be complicated especially if the items that are ordered by the client comes from different warehouses.

It is common for merchants sometimes to spend weeks contemplating on the rules that they have to make regarding shipping. One advice is this: implement a shipping policy that makes sense especially when the whole shipping expedition is considered. Since you are just starting out, take it slow. You will be formulating shipping policies that will make more sense in the future.

Shipping Internationally

Even though shipping internationally has changed drastically over the past years, it may still have some issues as compared to local shipping. If you want to ship internationally, here are just a few things that you have to consider:

- Additional charges from suppliers because most of them will have different rates when processing international orders.

- Higher shipping fees that may result in some problematic orders.

- There will be excessive costs especially if you have to ship items that are heavy.

- There are different limitations that should be considered depending on the country that you are going to ship to.

It will be up to you to decide if shipping internationally is actually worth it. It is not recommended when you are just starting out. You are always better off offering your business to local clients first. Who knows, probably in the future, you can offer to ship internationally.

Fulfilling the Order of Clients

It has already been discussed earlier that it is best to have more than one supplier as it allows you to ensure that all items will be in stock whenever people order but choosing the right suppliers that will help you run your company should be done with careful consideration. Some of the things that you should do are the following:

Choose suppliers based on location - It will still be easier if you would choose suppliers that will not have a hard time getting the products that you have ordered all the time. This means that if you have some customers that are within their route, you may choose them because of this reason alone.

Choose suppliers based on the items that they have available - You cannot force suppliers to have items in stock when they don't.

Choose suppliers based on price - It will be a nice idea if you can choose suppliers based on how they price their items but realistically, this is not possible because it will be complicated to figure out which supplier offers the best price.

Remember that as your business grows, the goal of suppliers is to give you the best items that you need. They will bid based on what your requirements are and usually, the one that bids the lowest will be chosen.

Picking the Carrier to Ship Items

The right carrier that can do the shipping for you will make a lot of difference with your business. Here are some carriers that you can consider:

1. US Postal Service - This may be the best carrier to choose if you are only shipping small items and if you are shipping internationally.

2. UPS/FedEx - They are well known for shipping large and heavy products locally, so you will not have any problems with hiring them for shipping large items.

Remember that when you are still creating options regarding your shipping, make sure that you will specify how long it will take before the products are sent. Choose the best choice for each order.

CHAPTER NINE

PROVIDING SUPPORT TO CUSTOMERS

Should You Offer Customer Support?

You may think that aside from managing all of the items that you receive from suppliers and talking to suppliers regarding the different things that they offer, focusing on managing your business and even providing customer support can be done easily. You are mistaken. You cannot do everything properly especially if you are just going to rely on yourself.

If you truly want to offer customer support, you may do this but make sure that you will assign someone else to provide the support that customers are searching for. If you do not want to hire an employee for that, you may want to implement a help desk instead. There are different help desk options available just choose the one that best fits your needs.

Should You Offer Phone Support?

There is a big possibility that there are some customers who are wondering if they can contact you through phone instead of their usual way of reaching you. This can be tricky because you may not be able to handle calls beyond your usual work hours. In case you have an employee whom you think will be able to handle the calls, then you can proceed by offering phone support to your customers. Just let your customers know what time they can call so they can reach your offered customer service support.

You should consider how you are going to advertise that you are already offering phone support. You may be tempted just to plaster it on your website especially if you have a number that is easy to remember but this can decrease the quality of the calls that you are going to get. There will be a lot of prank calls and calls that are not related to the items that you are selling at all. Place your number in places that only your loyal customers know about. This will improve the quality of your calls greatly.

You should also be prepared that there will be times when your customer needs to be appeased or to be contacted because of certain issues. If you have always hated speaking through phone, you have to put that aside in order to smooth out the problems. Always remember one rule when it comes to customer support: Never refuse to give your customers the help that they need when they need it.

CHAPTER TEN

A FEW THINGS TO REMEMBER TO SUCCEED

There are a lot of details that have been discussed so far and hopefully you have learned a lot about drop shipping and the different things that will help you run your own drop shipping company smoothly. You are supposed to have enough knowledge to be confident enough in building your own business.

The truth is told, however, there are still so many things that you have to consider so all of the facts may be hard to understand so far. Remember that it will be easy to forget about the most important things if you would not put it to heart and if you would not do what you are supposed to do.

There are some actions that you must do to ensure that your business will be a success. Here are just a few of the things that you can do:

1.   Do not forget to market your business.

You may become too busy thinking about the things that you have to do in order to make your business run smoothly that you will already forget to market your business. Marketing is easier now because of technology. Your main goal should be to drive people to come to your website. The more people who visit your site, the higher are the chances that you are going to have real customers whom you can serve.

You may be too focused on creating the perfect website. You are very meticulous about the details that you have used. In fact, you even took into consideration the colors that you will use for the different fonts as well as the images that you have placed on your website, but the moment that you launch it, you will realize that no one even knows that your website exists.

You can expect that during the first few months of your website, you will get zero traffic on your website unless you do something about it. Remember to give more than 3/4 of your effort to marketing. This can be more effective if you have already planned out how your business is going to be. You know that your business will go smoothly, but the main problem lies on how people will know what you are offering. If you do marketing correctly, you can already acknowledge some changes within 4 months.

Another thing that you have to focus on is your SEO. In order to improve your SEO ranking, you need to place the right content and the right keywords on your site. This can be a bit complicated to do especially without proper knowledge about SEO in general. The best thing to do is to hire a professional who can give the help that you need.

You always have a choice to learn everything on your own. You can learn how to do marketing, how to create your own website and how to do proper SEO but do you actually think that it is worth it? It may not be.

2.   Make sure that you have picked the right market.

You may be selling items that appeal to a certain market because it is the most popular. This may increase your chance of having a lot of customers, but at the same time, you cannot be sure if you will be noticed because of other drop shipping companies that offer similar things.

You know that with drop shipping, you are selling products but in order to stand out, you need to offer information and solutions to the problems of people. For example, if you want to reach people who tend to experience pain, you can offer products that will help get rid of that pain. You need to sell products that will improve your target market's quality of life.

The reason why you need to add value to the items that you sell is because if you would fail at doing this, your only option is to make your price lower than the rest of your competitors. You know what this means. The lower the price, the less profit you are going to make.

3.   Do not sell too many items all at once.

One of the mistakes that you are going to make when you are drop shipping is you will try to become a jack of all trades. You will assume that you can reach different target markets easily but is this true? Does this actually happen? When you sell too many items at once, you may appeal to different customers, but since you try to reach more than one target market, your items will tend to be limited towards a certain niche. For example, you may be selling books and toys, but you will not be selling as many books as another company that sells only books because you have toys to sell too.

It is okay to have more than one niche though if you are still starting out. This is because you are still trying to test the waters, you are trying to decipher what market you will lean towards more. Slowly but surely, you will get to understand which market you should sell more products too. When this happens, you can start pulling out the items that do not sell well and focus on those that do sell.

When you try to sell to a lot of customers all at once, it will make you seem like a "people pleaser, " and you know what happens to people pleasers, right? They usually end up being hated and ostracized because they try too much. You do not want your business to be labelled as such.

4.   Have a long term business plan

A lot of people usually think of having businesses as something that they will only do for a short period of time. For example, a person might decide to open a small business in order to earn enough money for the holidays, but when the holiday season ends, they will stop being active in doing their business already. If this is not your plan, then you should not act disinterested with your business plan? At the same time, you should have a planned, long term business plan that you will follow in the years to come.

You have to remember that in order for your business to become established, you would have to give it more than a year before it will flourish. It will take less than that if you would be good at doing marketing but if you are just a regular person trying to make your drop shipping business success, give it a year.

Be prepared that there will be days when you cannot help but become doubtful of the things that you have accomplished. Perhaps you may even think that you have not accomplished anything at all. It is likely that you will experience the following:

- Your website launch will be a dud.

- It will take time before people will start recognizing your website.

- You will not make sales immediately.

- You will have a lot of doubts about your business.

You will experience a lot of negative things, but you should be prepared and take it all in stride because it is all part of having a business. As long as you will be dedicated to giving the type of products and services that your customers need, your business will become a success eventually.

You should remember that only lottery winners and even casino jackpot winners get rich overnight. If you want to get your money the old fashioned way, you need to earn it one step at a time.

5.   The service that you give will always matter.

You should not only rely on your products in order to give you the success that you would like to achieve. You should focus on your services so that customers will keep coming back. In the past, people would need to talk to others regarding your business before it can become recognized but because of social media, sharing the service acquired from your company can spread like wildfire.

If you give poor service to one customer, you can expect that other people will know about it immediately through the customer's rants on his/her social media page. You may try to pacify the customer, but this does not always work. It can spell the end for your business when you are just starting out especially if you have committed a huge mistake.

Marketing has already been discussed earlier, and you know that SEO will help but the best marketing strategy is to make sure that all of your customers are satisfied. The more happy customers you have, the more that they will talk about your company and your products.

6.   Do not be too consumed by details.

Do you know why some business owners fail? It is because they become too focused on the little details of their business. They tend to focus too much on the logo of the company, the color of the font of the website and even the company's name. All of those things will matter, but there are other things that will matter more. You should not waste your time on these matters when there are a lot more things that you should focus on.

The moment that you have internalized all of the steps that are mentioned above, then there is only one thing left for you to do and that is, to start your business. A lot of people do careful planning that took them not only weeks but months to finalize only to realize in the end that there are some things that they are unhappy about so they do not push through with the business anymore.

You need to let go of your fears and reservations and start being serious about your drop shipping business because if you would not take it seriously, who will?

Conclusion

Well, there it is – what you need to know about using drop shipping as a means to start your retail business. In this book, we've looked at what drop shipping is, how it works and who is involved in the supply chain. We've also looked at how you need to select your niche and product and how to determine which suppliers are the best. I've given you the information you need to start your own business and what sales channels are available to you.

I hope that this book was helpful for you. Retail sales using drop shipping is a fairly common theme these days, so you need every edge you can get before you venture into this market. It is my hope that this book has provided you with at least some of those edges.

I hope you enjoyed reading this book. Do leave a review on Amazon and let me know what you think. Thank you!

Free Bonus: Join Our Book Club and Receive Free Gifts Instantly

Click Below For Your Bonus:

https://success321.leadpages.co/freebodymindsoul/

Checkout My Other Books

amazon FBA

STEP-BY-STEP GUIDE TO LAUNCHING YOUR PRIVATE LABEL PRODUCTS AND MAKING MONEY ON AMAZON

BEST SELLER

GREG ADDISON

http://amzn.to/2gf2ACP

www.ingramcontent.com/pod-product-compliance
Lightning Source LLC
Chambersburg PA
CBHW071445180526
45170CB00001B/471